Contents

Introduction

You may look different from your best friend on the outside, but inside you are both the same. The same body parts make up everybody — you, your parents, your friends and everyone else in the world.

Look at these faces. Can you see what makes each face look different and what makes them look the same?

Try pulling these faces in a mirror.

Happy   Cheeky   Sad   Surprised

Inside your body is a skeleton
like the one in this picture.
Everyone has a skeleton and
every skeleton looks the same.

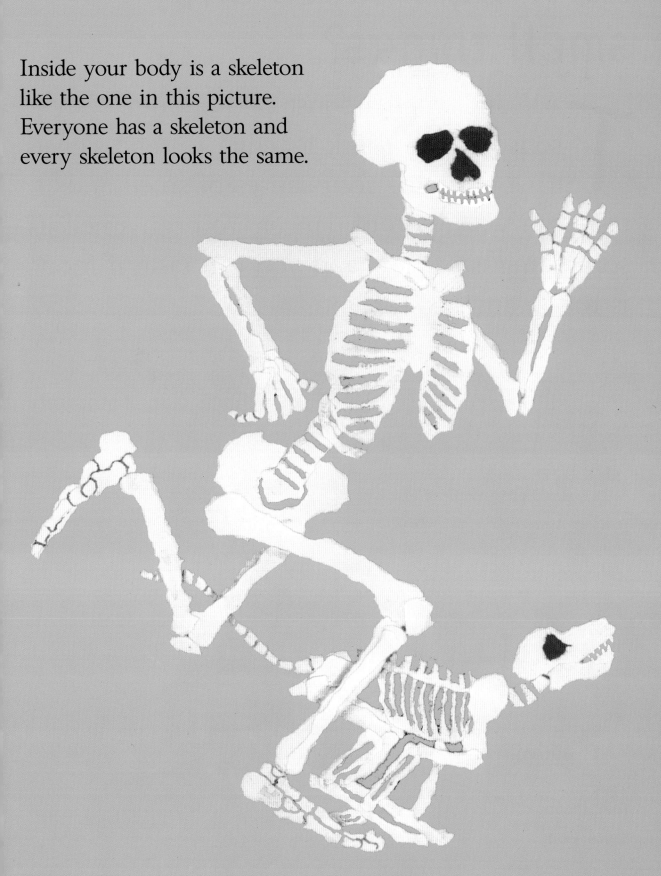

How do I taste and smell things?

Taste and smell are just two of your body's **senses**. They work together to send signals to your brain. Your senses of smell and taste can warn you of danger. You can smell if something is on fire, and you can taste if food is rotten and bad for you.

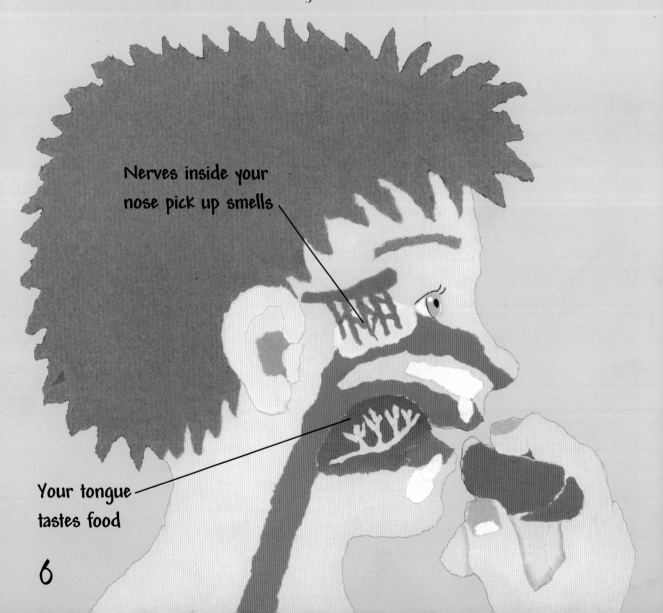

Nerves inside your nose pick up smells

Your tongue tastes food

Your tongue is covered with thousands of tiny **taste buds** that identify the different tastes in food and drink.

Different areas of your tongue taste different things.

Tastes can be bitter, sweet, salty or sour

bitter tastes at the back

sour tastes in the middle

salty and sweet tastes at the front

Five senses

Your body has senses of touch, taste, smell, sight and hearing.

It is harder to recognise tastes if you cannot see the food!

How do I hear and see?

Most of your ear is inside your head and you cannot see it. The part of the ear you can see is like a funnel for sounds.

When sound reaches your **eardrum** inside, it vibrates.

nerves

Vroom

Meeow!

Splash!

Bang!

Toot toot!

Crash!

Woof!

eardrum

As your eardrum vibrates, it sends messages to your brain which make sense of what you are hearing.

You see with your eyes. Light passes through your eye to a part called the **retina** at the back of your eye. Your retina sends the image of what you see to your brain.

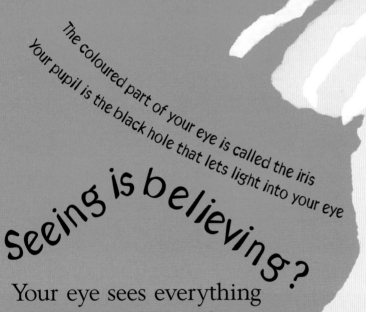

The coloured part of your eye is called the iris
Your pupil is the black hole that lets light into your eye

Seeing is believing?

Your eye sees everything upside down! Your brain then works out what you are looking at.

iris

pupil

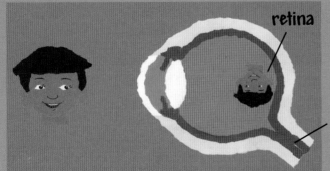

retina

Your optic nerve carries messages to your brain

9

Why do I have teeth?

You have teeth so that you can chew your food before you swallow it. Your first set of teeth are called **milk teeth**. Your milk teeth gradually fall out and bigger adult teeth grow in their place.

Children have 20 milk teeth. Adults have 32 teeth. How many do you have? Count them and see.

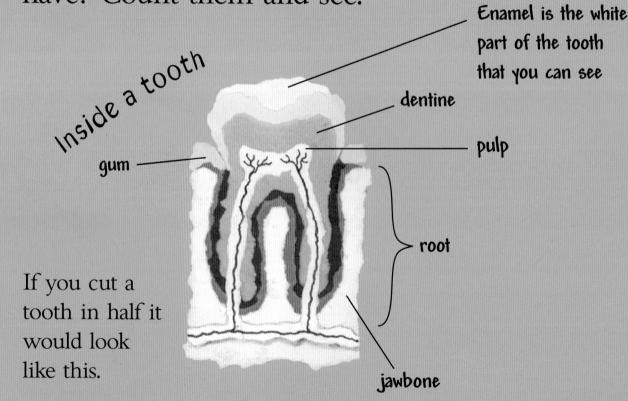

Inside a tooth

Enamel is the white part of the tooth that you can see

dentine

pulp

gum

root

jawbone

If you cut a tooth in half it would look like this.

You have different teeth for different uses. At the front of your mouth are **incisors** and **canines** for biting and tearing your food. At the back are big teeth called **molars** which crush and grind food.

Molars crush and grind

Canines are for tearing

Incisors are sharp for biting

Hold the page up to the light to see the skeleton.

Why do I have bones?

You have 206 bones in your body and each one has a different job to do. Bones make up your skeleton, which is what gives your body its shape.

Your bones are not very heavy. They are hard on the outside but spongy in the middle. The spongy part is filled with a jelly-like substance called **marrow**.

Your skull protects your brain

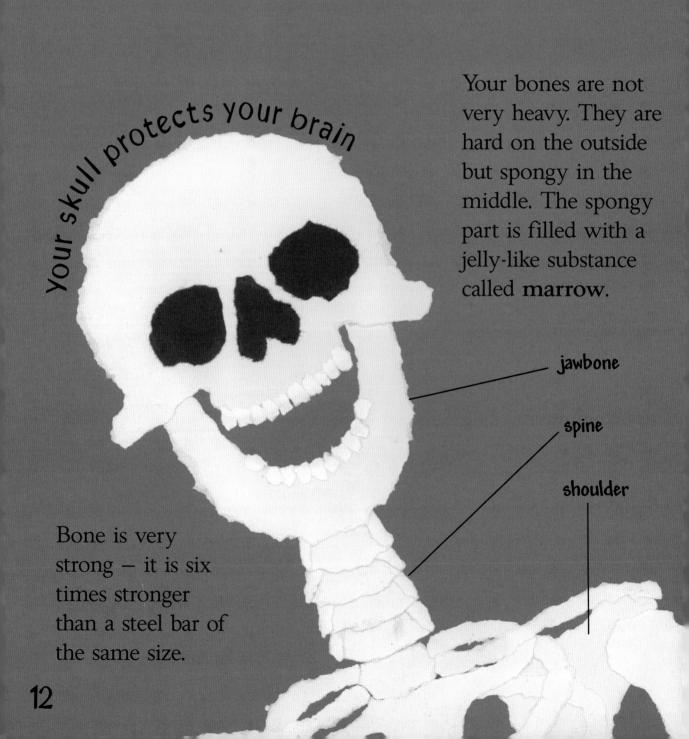

jawbone

spine

shoulder

Bone is very strong — it is six times stronger than a steel bar of the same size.

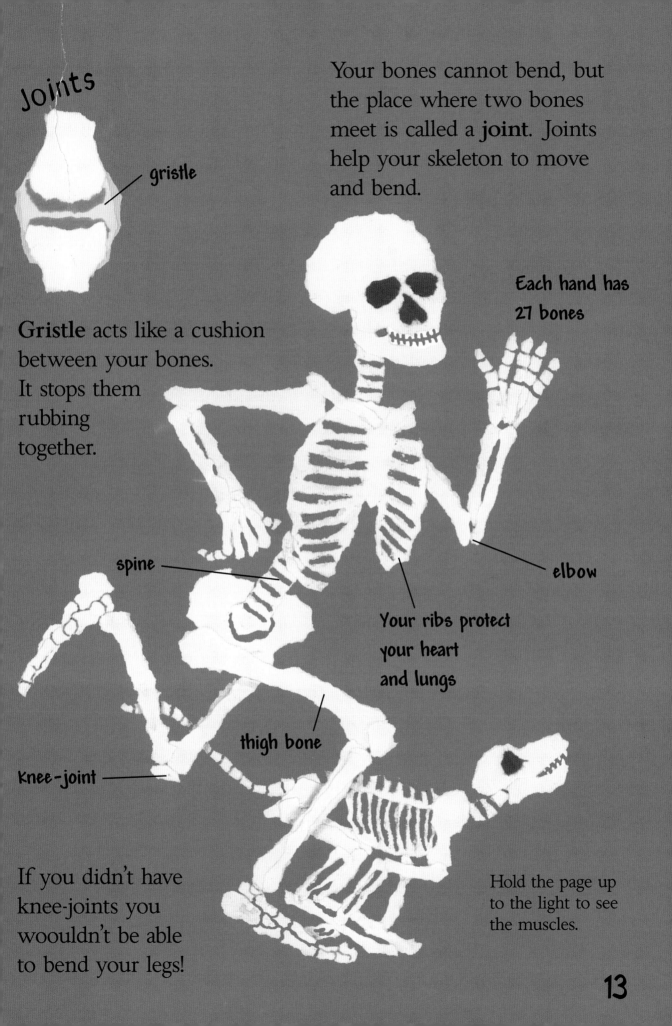

Joints

gristle

Your bones cannot bend, but the place where two bones meet is called a **joint**. Joints help your skeleton to move and bend.

Gristle acts like a cushion between your bones. It stops them rubbing together.

Each hand has 27 bones

spine

elbow

Your ribs protect your heart and lungs

thigh bone

Knee-joint

If you didn't have knee-joints you woouldn't be able to bend your legs!

Hold the page up to the light to see the muscles.

13

Why do I have muscles?

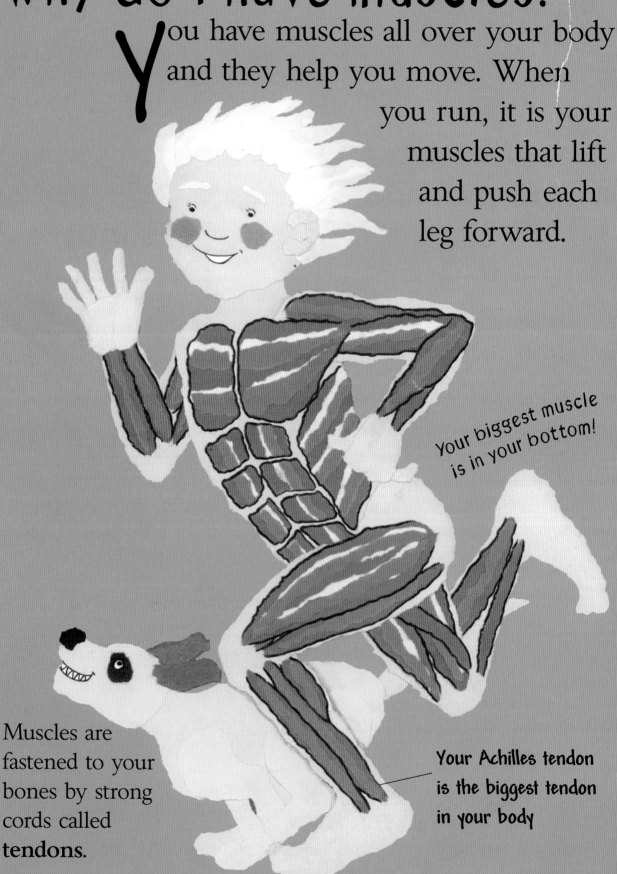

You have muscles all over your body and they help you move. When you run, it is your muscles that lift and push each leg forward.

Your biggest muscle is in your bottom!

Muscles are fastened to your bones by strong cords called tendons.

Your Achilles tendon is the biggest tendon in your body

You have around 600 muscles in your body

Most muscles work in pairs. As one muscle gets shorter, it makes the other muscle get longer.

This muscle (the biceps) gets shorter when you bend your arm

Try it for yourself. Hold out your arm and feel the big muscle (the biceps) on the top part of your arm. As you bend your arm upwards, you can feel this muscle getting harder and bigger as it gets shorter.

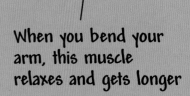

When you bend your arm, this muscle relaxes and gets longer

Why do I have skin?

Your skin covers your body and protects it. It helps to keep your 'insides' in, and keeps dirt and water out. It grows with you and it mends itself if you fall and graze your knees.

Your skin grows with you — it will always be a perfect fit

Not everyone's skin is the same colour. And some parts of your body have softer skin than others. Skin has **pores** — very small holes that let sweat out when your body gets too hot.

This close-up picture shows what you would see if you could look under your skin.

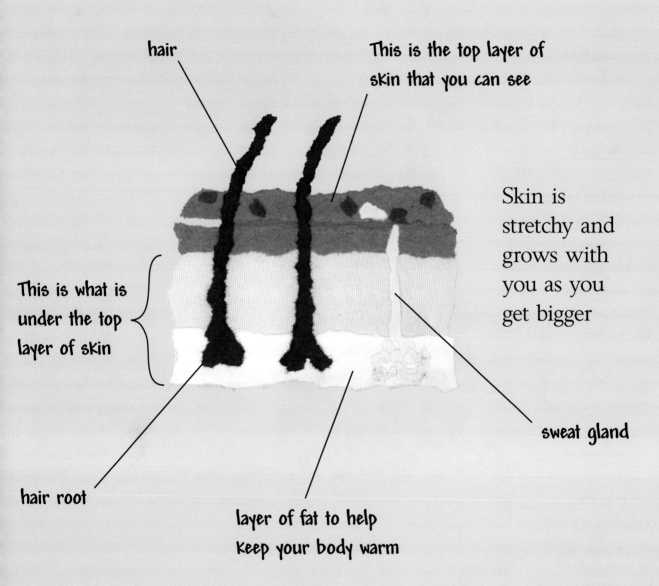

hair

This is the top layer of skin that you can see

Skin is stretchy and grows with you as you get bigger

This is what is under the top layer of skin

sweat gland

hair root

layer of fat to help keep your body warm

Tiny hairs grow all over your skin, except on your lips, the palms of your hands and the soles of your feet.

How does my stomach work?

When you bite into an apple, your teeth break it up into small pieces. As you swallow, these pieces slip down your foodpipe into your stomach.

Eat an apple

You chew food with your teeth before you swallow it.

Food gives your body energy.

foodpipe

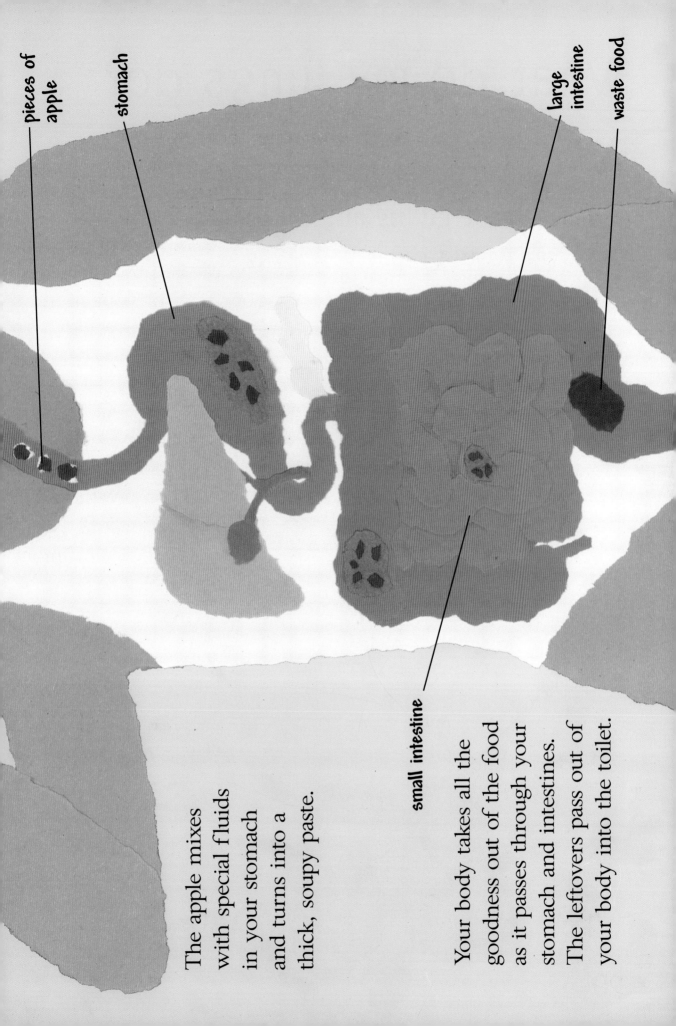

pieces of apple

stomach

large intestine

waste food

small intestine

The apple mixes with special fluids in your stomach and turns into a thick, soupy paste.

Your body takes all the goodness out of the food as it passes through your stomach and intestines. The leftovers pass out of your body into the toilet.

What do my lungs do?

You need lungs to breathe. Your lungs supply your body with life-giving air. Without air, you would die.

You can breathe through your nose or your mouth. Air goes down your **windpipe** into your lungs.

Air contains **oxygen**. As you breathe air into your lungs, oxygen is sent into your bloodstream.

lungs

windpipe

Air passages inside your lungs are like the branches of an upside-down tree

breathe **in** oxygen

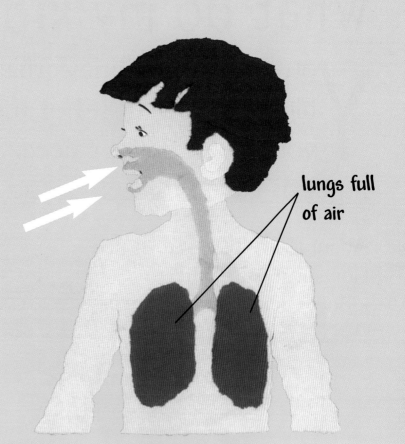

lungs full of air

You need oxygen to live. As you breathe in, your lungs fill up with oxygen-rich air. The air passages in your lungs take the oxygen into your body.

breathe **out** carbon dioxide

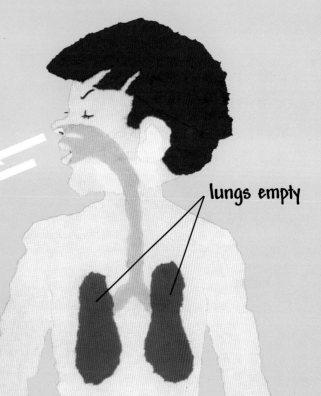

lungs empty

The air that you breathe out is called **carbon dioxide**. As you breathe out, your body gets rid of unwanted carbon dioxide.

What do my kidneys do?

You have two kidneys that clean your blood. They get rid of the things your body doesn't need. This waste liquid is called **urine**.

About a litre of blood flows through your kidneys every minute.

Urine travels from your kidneys and fills up your bladder. It passes out of your body into the toilet.

You have one bean-shaped kidney on the left and one on the right side of your body.

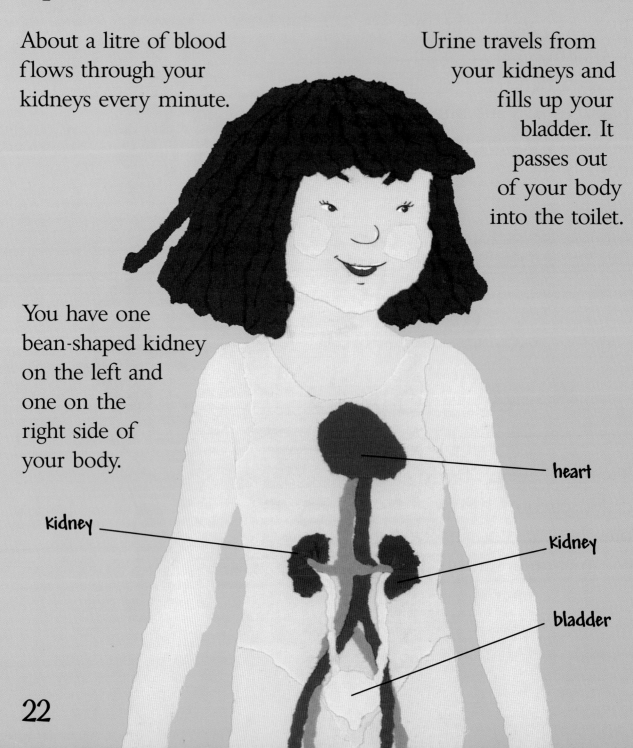

heart

kidney

kidney

bladder

What does my liver do?

Your liver does many different things. It makes a special fluid called **bile**. Bile helps to break down fat and old blood cells.

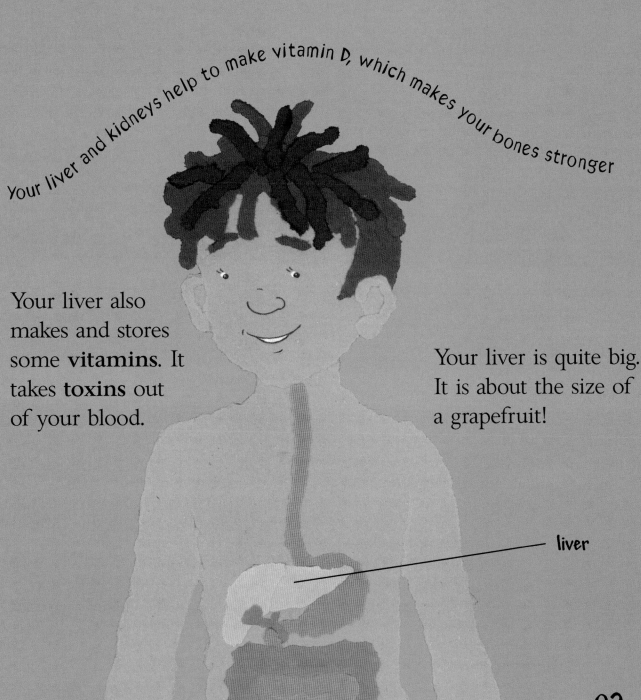

Your liver and kidneys help to make vitamin D, which makes your bones stronger

Your liver also makes and stores some **vitamins**. It takes **toxins** out of your blood.

Your liver is quite big. It is about the size of a grapefruit!

liver

What does my heart do?

Your heart is a muscle. It is about the size of your clenched fist. Your heart pumps blood to every part of your body. The blood is pumped through **arteries** and **veins.**

Press on the inside of your wrist. You should feel little movements like the beating of a drum. This is your pulse. It tells you how fast your heart is working to pump blood around your body.

To find out how fast your heart beats, count the pulse in your wrist for one full minute.

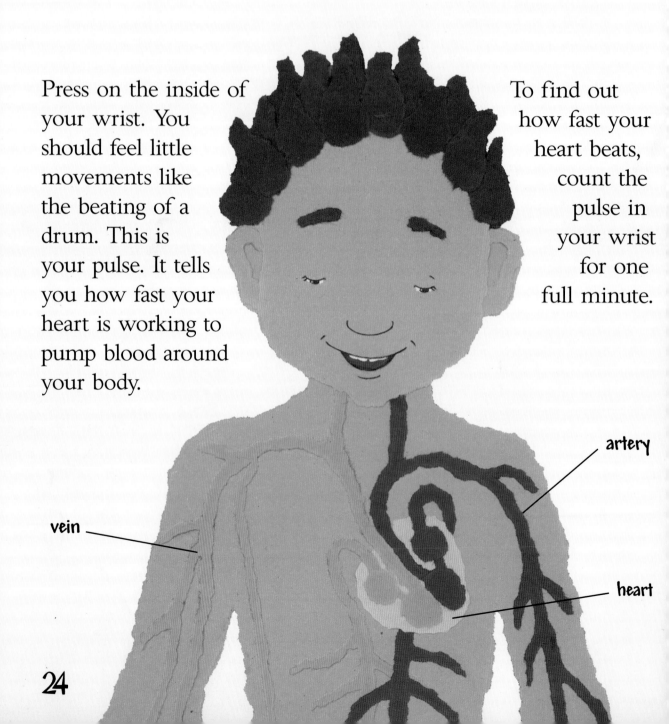

artery

vein

heart

Your body holds about five litres of blood!

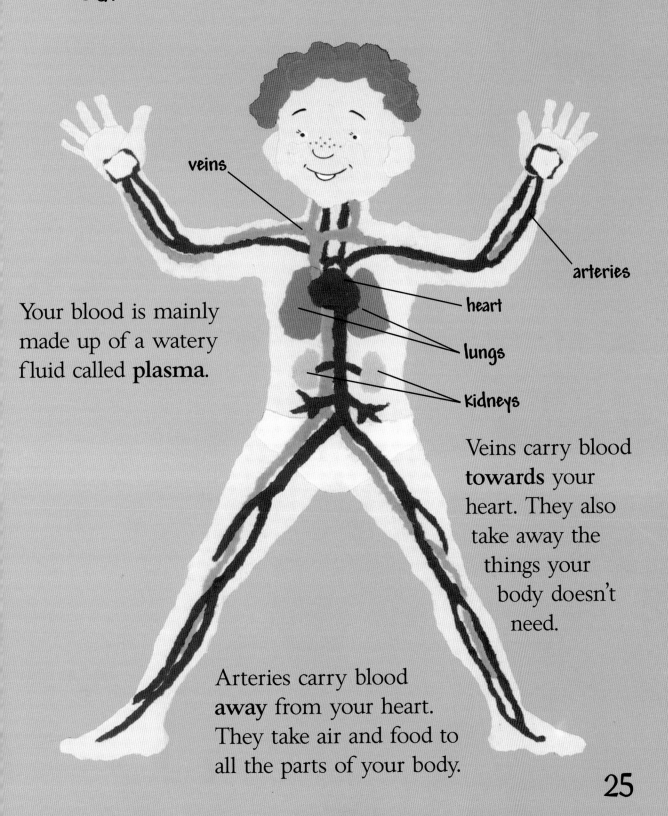

veins

arteries

heart

lungs

kidneys

Your blood is mainly made up of a watery fluid called **plasma**.

Veins carry blood **towards** your heart. They also take away the things your body doesn't need.

Arteries carry blood **away** from your heart. They take air and food to all the parts of your body.

How does my brain work?

Your brain is inside your skull. It is your body's computer. Your brain gets messages from around your body and decides what to do. It controls your thoughts, movements and memory.

Your brain weighs about the same as a bag of sugar

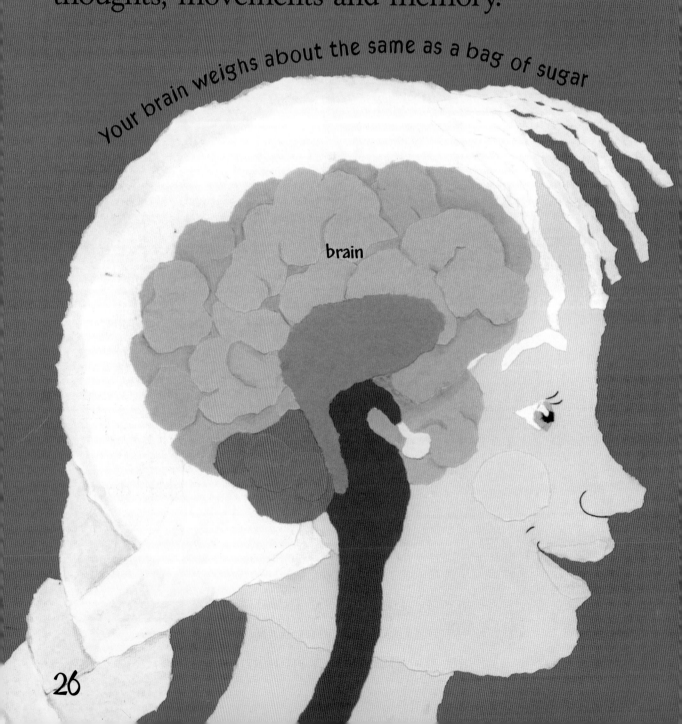

brain

When you see a ball
in the air, your brain sends
a message down your
spinal cord to your **nerves**.
Your nerves then send a
message to your muscles to
help you move and catch
the ball. This takes much
less than a second!

Your **spinal cord**
carries messages to your
brain from every nerve
in your body.

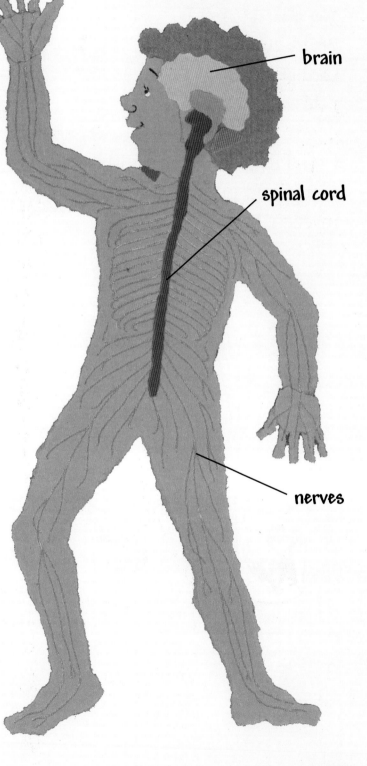

brain

spinal cord

nerves

You have nerves all over
your body sending all kinds
of messages to your brain.

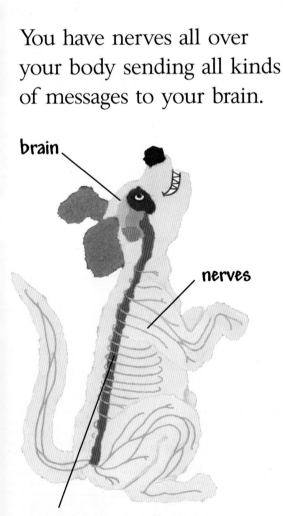

brain

nerves

spinal cord

Things to do

Feel the chill!

You will need:
Two glasses
Six ice cubes
Lard or fat (125 g)
Cold water

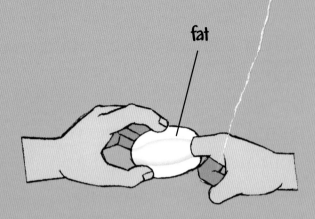

fat

1   Fill two glasses with water and put three ice cubes in each one.

2   Shape the fat into a ball. Carefully push one finger into the middle of the ball. Make sure your finger is completely covered by the fat.

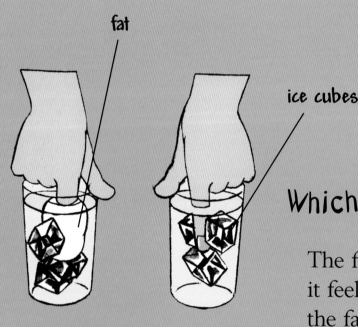

fat

ice cubes

Which finger feels coldest?

3   Put a finger in each glass of water.

The finger with the fat around it feels warmer! This is because the fat stops the skin on your finger feeling cold. The fat inside your body helps to keep you warm in the same way.

Seeing stars!

You will need:
Thin card (8 cm square)
2 lengths of wool (50 cm each)
One red and one blue felt-tip pen
Scissors

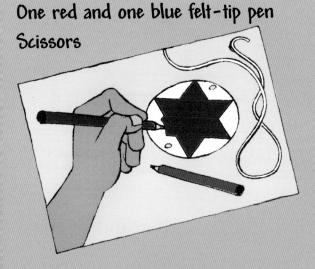

1   Ask an adult to help you cut a circle of card 8 cm in diameter. Draw a large star on one side of the card and colour it red.

2   Turn the card over and draw a small circle in the centre. Colour it blue.

3   Make a small hole on either side of the card and thread a loop of wool through each hole.

4   Put each loop around your thumb and forefinger and swing the circle round several times. When the wool is twisted tight, pull it in and out to make it spin.

What do you see?

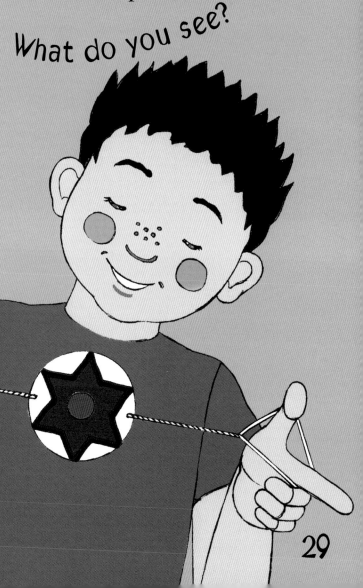

29

More things to do

You will need:

Plastic tubing (about 1 metre)

Plastic funnel

A friend

Listen to your friend's heart!

2 Ask your friend to put the open end of the funnel on the middle of their chest.

3 Put the other end of the tube to your ear.

1 Ask an adult to push the narrow end of the funnel into one end of the tubing.

What can you hear?

Words to remember

Bile A liquid made by your liver which helps to break down food.

Bladder A bag inside your body that holds urine until you go to the toilet.

Eardrum The part of your ear that vibrates when you hear sounds.

Intestines These long tubes help to digest food, absorb it into the body and get rid of waste.

Nerves Bundles of fibres which carry messages from different parts of your body to your brain.

Retina The part of your eye that responds to light. Your retina uses the optic nerve to pass messages to your brain about what you can see.

Senses The parts of the body that tell us what the outside world smells, sounds, feels, tastes and looks like.

Spine The long row of small bones that runs from the bottom of your back to the top of your neck.

Toxins Waste substances made by your body as it digests food and drink.

Vitamins Special substances found in food. You need vitamins to keep you healthy.

Index